Sumerian Vistas

By A. R. Ammons

Ommateum
Expressions of Sea Level
Corsons Inlet
Tape for the Turn of the Year
Northfield Poems
Selected Poems
Uplands
Briefings
Collected Poems: 1951–1971
(winner of the National Book Award for Poetry, 1973)
Sphere: The Form of a Motion
(winner of the 1973–1974 Bollingen Prize in Poetry)
Diversifications
The Snow Poems
Highgate Road
The Selected Poems: 1951–1977
Selected Longer Poems
A Coast of Trees
(winner of the National Book Critics Circle Award for Poetry, 1981)
Worldly Hopes
Lake Effect Country
The Selected Poems: Expanded Edition

Sumerian Vistas

Poems

••

A. R. AMMONS

W · W · NORTON & COMPANY

NEW YORK   LONDON

Published simultaneously in Canada by Penguin Books Canada Ltd.,
2801 John Street, Markham, Ontario L3R 1B4.
Printed in the United States of America.

The text of this book is composed in Janson.
Composition and manufacturing by the Maple-Vail Book Manufacturing Group.

First Edition

ISBN 0-393-02468-7

ISBN 0-393-30425-6 pbk.

W. W. Norton & Company, Inc., 500 Fifth Avenue, New York, N.Y. 10110
W. W. Norton & Company Ltd., 37 Great Russell Street, London WC1B 3NU

1 2 3 4 5 6 7 8 9 0

Acknowledgments

Certain of the poems included here first appeared in *Bound*, *The Carolina Quarterly*, *The Cornell Alumni News*, *Epoch*, *The Nation*, *The New Yorker*, *The Poetry Miscellany*, and *The Raritan Review*. "The Ridge Farm" was first published in *The Hudson Review*. My deep thanks to the editors. A good many of the poems first appeared in a special issue of *Pembroke Magazine*, edited by Shelby Stephenson, to whom I am warmly grateful.

David Burak, Augustus Carleton, Roald Hoffmann, and Phyllis Janowitz read and gave me comments on many of the poems. "The Ridge Farm" was selected largely by Jerald Bullis from a longer version. I am deeply indebted for his help.

I am grateful to many unknown to me, those who nominated me and recommended me for a MacArthur Fellowship. I humbly acknowledge the generosity of the MacArthur Foundation and the kindness and consideration of those who administered my award.

for Phyllis & John

Contents

1 THE RIDGE FARM

1

The lean, far-reaching, hung-over sway
of the cedars this morning!
vexed by the wind and working tight

but the snow's packed in, wet-set,
and puffed solid: the cedars nod to
an average under gusts and blusters:

yesterday afternoon cleared the
sunset side of trees, the hemlocks
especially, limbering loose, but
the morning side, the lee, sunless
again today, overbalances:

the grackles form long strings
of trying to sit still; they weight
down the wagging branchwork snow stuck
branch to branch, tree to shrub,
imposing weeds

2

last night, the wind clunked
the icy heads of shrubs
against the house—
a long night of chunk-money spilling

3

a poet hands me his poem and says,
this is not my true voice, only a
line or so:
good, I say, but he is
disappointed,
having found a self, if still reticent,
in himself he likes or would like to like:
but is his true
voice more interesting
than the one in the poem and, anyway,
isn't the one in the poem, if untrue,
truly untrue:
I know what he means:
he wants to write by the voice, to
separate out the distinctive
in himself, a distinctive, and write to it:
that is not the way, the way
is to say what you have to say
and let the voice find itself
assimilated from the many tones and sources, its
predominant and subsidiary motions
not cut away from the gatherings:
but that is passive, he says:
no, I retort (for effect), it is passive
to do the bidding of the voice you have
imagined formed: freedom engages,
or chooses not to, what in the world is
to be engaged

4

if nature could speak
would it have something
to say right where it says nothing:
that is, be like me, reticent,
patient, waiting and slowly the

progressions will find progressive gears
(even now backsteppings are being wound
forward) and the wind seek key other
than the eaves-key: nature would say,
be still, that is to say, indifferent
like me, only to say so would
motion difference:
probably this is why nature says nothing—
it has nothing to say

5

knowledge, perception, this action
is so endless it might well be
avoided, as one does not care to take
down just because it happens what happens, the play
of light on an inlet, bay, sea:

worked so far in, knowledge mingles
with its source
so as to give up reefs, shoals, shores
of resistance, to unwind
the embracing curvatures of line,
shelf, lagoon

recalcitrance, fluency: these:
too far with one and the density
darkens, the mix slows, and bound
up with hindrance, unyielding, stops:
too far with the other and the bright
spiel of light spins substanceless
descriptions of motion—

always to be held free this way,
staggering, jouncing, testing the
middle mix,
the rigid line of the free and easy

there is no tedium, apparently,
to mere things in eternity: sunset,
now underway with rosy ruffles,
deep glows becoming space effects,
all that, so fresh and vanishing,
so old, the sun itself simultaneously
setting and rising continuously
on this or that sea or mountain range,
gorilla troop or small nation: Lord
God, I cry out (hear me), hear us:
but the Lord God changes before our minds
and becomes a listening device
four warps and a reach (woof) deep into
space: we cry out, bending an umbrella
of focus His way to penetrate
nothingness, signals, arbitrary, noticeable, intelligible

7

some branches, the
birch's, end bushy
but the squirrel,
no aerial rail to catch, will
leap into the vague
net and, bounding, find
route to hard wood

8

we went for a raw walk in the
high middling of the afternoon, the
wind getting into and up our coats
and even gently into our pants:
nevertheless, we would not be daunted,
the rain also, though sparsely and
smallishly, prickling us, it being

forced forward stingingly by the gusts:
the evergreens and clouds rolled:
we heard the tough, rattling burr of
highwind in the hardwoods and the softer muffle
of cedar boughs: we noticed the
forsythia standing half-out: we
noticed the honeysucklebushes filled
with tiny green lotus temples where last
week ice had hung cold-dry or rattled loose:
Bernie said he wasn't much interested
in nature but if we didn't have it we'd have to
think of something to take its place

cauliflowers are either real or
illusory, ditchbanks shed inward into their
courses old cattail fuzz, fern
fiddleheads, sporophyte flimsy either
appearance or verifiability:
gravy runs down the chin and forms
brothy drops that can't or can favor stain:
why test mind on the reality stone:
nothing will be determined but that
mind, too, terribly flows and stalls, holds
and gives way: if you don't
eat the imaginary potato (grown in an
imaginary field, baked in an imaginary
oven) your real capacity
to imagine illusion lessens:

hug thighs to thighs, sit broken with clarity
of delight at children
in the early afternoon sun, hold
on to some specification of curvature
the "flavor" of a mind that once informed
a love face, let nothing vanish that has not
proved out a firm roundaway

miss the kingdom of feelings
or find it too much and it is
indifferent who made the world or what
it was made of, stone or vision

10

the clumps and small reservoirs of
snow (as in forks of big trees where
honeysucklebush sometimes starts or
moss or fern finds aerial pond)
are gone and no rain
worth troubling the soil has fallen
lately: the early morning brook is dark,
its rock shale bottom showing through,
the water dawn-clear at last, filtered
black diamonds: the stump of a giant
dutch elm stands by: its bark warps
off in swales of curvature: splits
enter radially closer
and closer to the heart: the meat
mush-sodden feeds mushrooms, big
whiteheaded, and brackets respond
vigorously to the softening:
various mechanisms appropriate,
necessary, useful, even beautiful
will do away with it in time and then
the mechanisms will find other work,
earth's supply of dutch elm stumps run out

11

rather than the play of the mind as
wind on tidal or other creeks or
streams or even runlets developed in
gravel by macadamways, why not
dwell the mind on mushrooms till the several

kinds define themselves, select their habitats,
go through a few life cycles, and reach their
roots into where they come from and
of what and how they go and get
back from there: attend to mushrooms and
all other things will answer up:
while if you flick off (leaping like light)
all the scallops of a broad scape to keep it
noted and active, you may not in your own
summaries add much up

12

how to exclude the central,
exclusive reductions, the narratives
that consume the environment
transparent into their symmetries:
how to get out into the looser
peripheries where the roots of
specific trees hold them away from
the maelstrom and birds
have occasion to fly: but, of
course, not too far out, away, from
the controlling knots

everything is established, even all
the motions: even the revolutions
turn with the gears of necessity
and even the little motion that
gets away into some lost or possible
refiguring is figured on: there is
no cause for alarm: and no joy except
in buying everything

13

I like the ridge, its rolls my fixed ocean:
not *my*, I don't own an inch of it:
and not theirs, either, the ones who
do own it, for they don't see it or
their part in it:
I'm part of the ridge they see in the
east, their morning place: nearly in
the height of the summits around here
I see the sun come out of flat
land, nearly, lingeringly interfered
with by ordinary trees: for evening
though the sun has gained space over
the lake, its setting among trees
no more than fuzz from here: it
encounters rockswales sharp on:
fire and stone flare together and the fluid
yields and sinks past, burning, darkened, out:
but I like the ridge: it was a line
in the minds of hundreds of generations
of cold Indians: and it was there
approximately then what it is now
five hundred years ago when the white
man was a whisper on the continent:
it is what I come up against:
it regularizes my mind though it has
nothing to do with me intentionally:
the shows that arise in and afflict
nature and man seem papery and
wrong when wind or time tears
through them, they seem not only
unrealistic but unreal: the ridge,
showless, summary beyond the trappings
of coming and going, provides a
measure, almost too much measure,
that nearly blinds away the present's
fragile joys from more durable woes

14

I've had all the apples out of my
basket (or tossed them out, whole
or spotty-rotten) I couldn't
wait to see the empty basket,
light, structurally transcendent:
but some mornings I get up and can
make nothing of it: it is empty:
I fall into it and vanish: other
mornings it is the very starvation
I have longed for so long to chide
and mock the world with:

but then it is a wastebasket and I
put it out to the use of the world:
it collects trash of the thoughty:
others (the litter litterers) give
theirs to the wind, the chance and
random boys: but I don't think
there's much distinction between
saved and spent trash: trash is what
you make of it: if you throw it away
you are rid of the problem—unless
a little bit is waiting to greet you
your next day round: and there is
no way, of course, finally to
throw anything away to

15

considering mutability and muck,
transforming compositions and
decompositions, ups and downs, comings
and goings, you have, sir, passed
from a thousand orifices, some
beneath you on the evolutionary
scale: visibly moved, the gentleman

11

got some roll-on ban deodorant
and tried to rub me off (or out):
shit sticks: its fragrance in the old
days confirmed the caveman he was coming
home: a man's shit (or tribe's) reflects
(nasally) the physical makeup of the man
and the physiologies of those others
present, plus what they have gathered
from the environment
to pass through themselves

the odor of shit is like language,
an unmistakable assimilation of a
use, tone, flavor, accent hard to
fake: enemy shit smells like the enemy:
everything is more nearly incredible
than you thought at first

16

nature that roots under us
thrusting us up and out
flows through assembling
us but eventually
the structures of the mouth
crack down to incontinent corners
moist, the eyes weeping
air's mere burn

(the waste in a woods gives
off the best heat and brightest
illumination: all growing is
gourd green: but the fallen
lie about dry and light, lightwood,
ready at a click of fire to
rage response, its fast undoing its
best revelation)

flows through
taking us apart, returning fine knots
to recycling's fuzzy frays
and chunks: can we not,
then, find in these majestic
necessities
room for consideration,
notice of the sacred, an
overriding working steady
in care and keeping: look
elsewhere or go on paying close attention

sap, brook, glacier, spirit
flowing, these are sacred but
in a more majestic aloofness
than we can know or reason with:
we can participate in it only
imaginatively, even as we are
assembling to prevent the giving
way under us: a sacredness above
the sacredness we needed, which
would direct some arc, preferably
a towering tower, some band or
quality of concern to
recognize us here in the
first case, being concerned,
different by that concern
but we should not expect
easy sacredness that
turns aside to us when we wish
and leaves us alone to whole joys: we should
expect that the sacred, too, will
try, elude, abandon us
so as to show something
high to realize, recalcitrant,
unyielding to makeshift in
its quality, something we could

miss altogether even while it
sustained us throughout until the
carrying off or away

we assemble the variable materials until
balance begins
defining out, then we explore the
validity of the balance, collecting and
testing in cooperation with it, then
its fullness approaching satisfactory
disposition, we test it down to see if
it can give or crack: if it holds we
come into a high, intricate consideration
of the balance, the branches and
embranchments so fine, the recalcitrant
solidity of the mass or number and
justice begins to appear, the distance
that lets the wolf run and kill and the
caribou mosey on: starved crows
showing up for hide shreds: the wolverine
cagey, careful, capable on the
periphery of astonishing kills:
snow eaten for blood salt: so
many things to consider, undoing so
unlikely, assent follows, the wide band
of the mind shifting to acceptance,
finding the staying place amid
horror, lust, need, necessity, that
which is, a small
place to walk in a system of others

17

we live again in the bellies
of worms, fly again (?) with
winged worms: we come sponging
back to the tables of our children

to be swatted: since this
is one place,
going is coming, ending beginning,
individual shape shed
like exoskeletons of spiritual flies

18

I go to nature not because
its flowers and sunsets speak
to me (though they do) or
listen to me inquire but

because I have filled it with
unintentionality, so that I
can miss anything personal in
the roar of sunset, so that

I can in beds of flowers hold
my head up, too: whereas,
the forms of intention, the
faces swept chill-firm with conviction

can assemble and roll down
streets and declare divisions
that save or kill: I go to
nature because man is scary,

his mercilessness not like
the jaguar's which can be evaded
but like one's own mercilessness,
inescapable as one's own intellect

and devising, the mercilessness
from which there is no appeal

19

I wouldn't give up a hair of
the beautiful

high suasions of language,
celestial swales, hungering the
earth up into heaven, no,
I would just implicate
the language with barklike beeps,
floppy turf
of songsound, I would lift up so much
of the whatnot
it would pull the heavens down
commingling with things and us

I would give up nothing
if I had my way: I would just
idle a belt or two of trees over here
a while and turn aside a river or
so there, and keep a few continents
waiting a second, and I would
go from one thing to another until
I had the impression I could tell what
was going on and I would sing it all
up, like lassoing, and tie it down

20

when the hand falls apart it makes
a handful of bones, a
spill or smallest cairn: no matter
how much the hand taught
of love or how many times it flew
upward to catch the raiments of heads
of hair or how busy it seemed in water
quick fish or how it was the strongest
shoal many a death could reach or how
much it seemed to assume the forms of
its tasks
here it is now a fact, neutral,
plain, open for inspection, the cutest

collection, a peak white as a
peak tip, take some into your hands,
take them with you, hold them up to the light
to see, roll them, throw them,
conjure up the wind's chances with them

21

heaven can be as purified as your
consciousness demands, I suppose, but
think of a heaven with people only in it,
gorillas missing, not worthy of soul,
but if all things are soulful and kept
why then will we meet as well as our
old friends the chickens we've killed
and / or eaten, sows and piglets, shoats
and boars and other animals, quite
an extensive catalog in our freezers and
refrigerators, will they be there grunting
at us or, indeed, rushing
us, gobbling our souls up

22

once you've caught the notion,
perceived the evidence, raked it
up, sorted through it, the recurrent
from the fortuitous, meanwhile casting
out the merely repetitious, bundled
sortings up, clumped certain ones into
bags, tied strings around the bags,
heaved the whole business up on your
shoulders and jostled around till
you've found the balance point in
it—what an amazement
as you stand there searching stillness,
not yet having decided where to go

with it all, if anywhere, to realize
that the balance, the point of
balance, is a found piece of permanence
in the disposition of things (look how
many *of*'s), a still place, primordial
form, and that every shiftless thing
it took to find
the point is mere change's shifting

23

slice thirty degrees off the summer
summit eighty and the windy ridge
that's left can change your summer
clothes: it's April and
glory is still uncertain and death
not:
  the air is so clear and the
  sky fine blue this morning,
  small showers having given
  fringes to the front coming
  through last night:
a V of about forty geese, late,
and working nearly into the NW
wind, struggled through, haggling:
I've seen geese that waited early
for the right high wind go over
like they were skating, the wings'
strokes covering apparent distances
(real distances, but not real air
distances) only gliding could acct for

24

last year we got this strawberry
jar, a ceramic bulge-bellied vase with open
ears all around it and a strawberry plant

growing in each ear: winter came and I
put the affliction in the garage where
naturally the temperature fell below
zero, though sometime during the day
the window found a ray that caught
the jar (not warming it much): the leaves,
cold-scorched quickly dead, remained green
all winter but when put out this
spring turned burnt brown, you can just
imagine:
   this story is too short for a long
      story and too long for a short story:
      anyway, today I observed two green serrated
      feelers oozing up into each of two ears
      and thought to my self "my word"
the plants didn't die: by then, that is
by this morning, since I had thought the
plants dead and stopped watering them,
the jar was shrunk dry: so I went to
get the plastic wateringcan that has
been sitting all winter under the outside
faucet catching, since thaw, drops: leaks:
I noticed last fall's leaves in the
can and thought well that will improve
the juice but I thought it did smell
funny: I poured water into the jar-top
and most of it, drought-refused, ran over or
out: so I waited for the soak to take and
began to think something really
smelled: I poured some more rich brown
juice into the jar and then upended
the can to let the leaves fall out and
out plunked this animal clothed in
leaves so I couldn't tell what he was
except his thick tail looked thicker
than a rat's: mercy: I'd just had
lunch: squooshy ice cream: I nearly

unhad it: I expect the crows will come
and peck it up, up, and away, the way
they do squirrels killed on the
streets: pulling at the long, small
intestines and getting a toehold on
small limbs to tear off the big flesh

25

the rat was a mole: the arctic air
yesterday afternoon dried him out and
the freeze last night stiffened him much
reduced in size and scent: so
I broke out the shovel, dug up a
spade, dumped in the mole: there let
him rot, the rat: I can see how
something blind could get into my
wateringcan: but with those feet!
I can hear him scratching up the side:
to get in, or out: but also I can hear him
sloshing, the blind water darkened by
night, till nobody came

26

there is something about
a redbird flying down
into
the brook bed, the stone-deep ditch,
and lighting on a washed-out root,
the brook meanwhile throwing mirrors
everywhere—light, mirror, bird, stone

27

I like, as I have said before,
maximum implication and

registration of fact and tension before
integration catches on as to how

it is to work and the point it
catches on to the finish what a war

between what will and will not be
captured by design, bent to a larger

rule, made to serve, expand, elaborate:
it is not right until the design

at once insists on itself and accommodates
itself to the material all the way out

to the tricky coincidental! for if
the central, controlling design will

not submit to the chippy alteration of
the surprising appearance, the fortuitous

bit, its control will be perfect, a
nonplace, emptiness: but the integration

that tests itself, adjusting, sorting,
out to the limit why it holds because

there is nothing to loosen it, garrisons
and amassings of questioning having
meanwhile overturned the perfect

28

it doesn't matter to me if issues
overload a line:
or if real poetry shrugs shucking
bugs of small intentions
off the shoulders of its purer
streams—what the fuck—everybody
has to eat, nature overfilling

everything to fill it:
yesterday was one day, today is
another, tomorrow still one more:
the creeps:
the sun is bright but can never
squint fine enough to count time
by my span:
it is unavailing: everyone knows
that when we die we wake up
elsewhere from the dream life into
life, hop over a fence and
walk off across nobody's pasture

29

I wake from a nap
in a room I have worked
so many hours and years
in, made long poems &
dinky ones in, read and
answered letters and
thrown some out unread
or unsent and I cannot
remember ever having been
here before, this place,
the woods
out the window, what does
it mean, and then I recall
a trace, but nothing I
couldn't throw away, and
that trace fits with a
recent time that blocks
out into fullness of
being and then the walls
settle, the house
takes disposition
with the street, the

town, oh, yes, the lake, ridges,
I yawn a couple of times
and pick up the latest
thing to do

30

words cast up
to see if light
will pick anything out in them

like sand and trash
a winnowing:
though I cast up true

words as far as I know
(words that truly
occur) I cannot be

held wrong when I range
into winnowing chaff,
truly chaff: I am

seeing: I am looking to make
arrangements: is the land
rich, are the children

well, the mind, is it
well-stocked and with what,
fish: has a grain

of hope or grain been
found: is there, going
this way or that, any

increase in increase or
any falling off: is, at
this time, any direction

worth finding: I said
the words in the time
of themselves: I said the

words as truly as I could
say them, according to
themselves: the words

are not responsible: they
are not the truth: they
caught the swerve, they

revealed the glint: the
mind opens—it is so
delightful, glaring—many

times before it finds a
room worth finding:
but chaff will show

you "which way the wind
blows" truly: my words
are, of course, chaff

as assertions are:
but the motions: as
the wind blows, so blows

the world: in the
innerwork of the
motions one reads what will

be aright and turns here or
there as he can (ashcan) to get
away or be there with it:

I speak to show not
the substance but
the curvature of the going

the substance may change often
but the curvature has a glacial
pace, seeming, to tell the truth,

out of kilter with substance:
but probably, though we can't
wait too long to see, it comes
out right eventually

31

I was this
morning affrighted past loafing
by the small blood
lining the squirrel's mouth
where he lay on the highway's edge
his legs spraddled stiff into space
the high eye full of the morning sun
the other
scrinching wide open on grainy macadam

oh, me, I said, myself affected, cars
are our worst predators
getting more
than crows can hawk (hocking &
spitting) into shreds even
(though it's good
that some things clear things away—
in the old caves

dying men
shoved into backroom fissures, split trenches,
found quickened way to rigid ease)

a young couple bicycling came up the
hill past the squirrel and though the
girl's eyes cast it a slight shake
her talk didn't break and they went on
by with the tribute of being glad to get
by:

the car itself, the kill recent, had
gone on, notifying no one—why notify,
or how, a different species: we never
tell mules we're dead, though they say
Uncle Asa's great-horned owl knew the
afternoon, changing, he died because his
hooting skirled or whatever and he
wouldn't stop moaning, the thriving
throat croak, and dogs out under the
lean-to's of barns know when their
masters lie dying

32

today Jerry, Fran, Phyllis and I went
to see the high farm out by Mecklenberg:
the farm starts high and keeps getting
higher: the brook runs way up and
on the way is the low pond but further
up, the larger high pond and then
there are a couple of fields of
ascension and then the old woods of
the ridge, precipitous in climb, not
available to hassling lumbermen:
along the ridge is a long march
you don't have to sweat once you're

there: wild turkey, deer, grouse
inhabit the inaccessibilities and make
do: I would buy a whole 130-acre farm
for one hermit lark, his song,
especially his song at evening by a
pond: right now there are some shabby
sheep, eight cocks (henless): I heard
one cock crow, a sound I've been as hungry
for as the lean throats of cockerels:
one dog, the master not around, three or four
scrubby cattle: an apple tree a hundred
years old looking better in spring
leaf than the house a hundred years
old: it's got so the only place you
can appreciate won't appreciate: the
silence was ineluctable: I heard it
& heard it: it reminded me of the
ground: noise is motion: silence
deepens down and picks up ground
boulders and deepens down to springwater

33

I'm split but not
in two, I bough
into ramification,
I break out into
peripheries of leaf,
mist informs my
rondures: I go more
than halfway one way
and crosslash back
away: my
splits overlace:
the complication
strengthens me,
interweaving my

27

fragmentation, so
that I include
in a sweep of singleness
as much singleness
as one needs and
more than enough
sweep

34

don't think we don't
know one breaks
form open because he fears
its bearing in on him
(of what, the accusation,
the shape of his eros, error,
his guilt he must buy
costing himself)
and one hugs form because
he fears dissolution, openness,
we know, we know:
one needs stanzas to take
sharp interest in and
one interests the stanza
down the road to the wilderness:
life, life: because it is
all one it must be divided
and because it is
divided it must be all one

35

wherever mortality sets up a net
or responsibility's strictures harden
I mount into a whirlwind and
buzz off, clearing a streak
I spend the night in sonnets but the

next morning pack my bag with free verse
the road is my winding song sheet
the rivers, branches, brooks purl
my uneasy pleasures:
leaving everything behind, I stick to
nothing
I will not hear the terms of arraignment
or appear in the marble courts
I will not bear the sophistry,
subtle ramification, of the arguments
for and against:
yet the guilt sharp as jails has gotten through:
the air dissolves and absorbs,
oceans dissolve and absorb,
the imagination changes things
whose change, the hell of things, comforts me

36

straitened narrow, river-wound
through the pass, bluff walls misty
with moss-like trees,

doing what is worth doing is worth
what doing it is worth
but doing what is not worth doing
that can really be worth doing
often when one is denied access
to reality
imagination will rise to the occasion
and body
forth the vivid thing as if itself
so the deprived
may be given all but touch of the
form, color, line

or will produce the very presence of
the thingitself itself but with
shadowy reservation to please the mind
but not the solid body

lawn full of goldfinches eating
dandelion seeds, the headful whipped
over, held by a perchfoot—the yellows
nearly interchangeable

37

everyone watches the world end once
or if one is asleep
the roots of his dreams loosen and
brain soil crumbles down the slopes
or if a coma has risen right into the
shallowest waters of awareness
why then the world may as a skim of light end

38

I don't care if I don't tell the truth
the she-spider hangs to the ceiling
of the backporch as if, dead since last
November, alive: by her hang five
egg sacs, waiting: the she-spider
flares there, dead and dry, guarding still:
or I don't care if I tell the truth
the way the struck squirrel in his fifth
day by the roadside begins with perfect
accuracy to advertise his whereabouts: the truth
is none of my business: I don't care if
I tell a little: my business is to make
room for the truth, to bust the couplet,
warp the quatrain, explode the sonnet,
tear down the curvatures of the lengthy:

the truth is commodious, abundant: we
must make a room so sufficient it will
include till nothing will be left
over for walls, merely the thinning away
to the numb, great vacancy visible

39

in the small walks & chasms
of despair one seeks to find and
pretends to build enledgments to
plateaus of staying and view but
these unfound, pretended become high
lake surfaces of chagrin, false, of
course, in themselves but,
worse, too brilliant for common use

40

the honeysucklebushes already weighty
with new leaf and blossoms can hardly
bear the most recent foliage, snow:

the branches separate in the dome and
fall all ways, in the angle of falling
catchment for snow amply provided,

the bent bent, the bush crushed,
a great ground flower:
                              the desert

mouse twitches under the rule of the
rattler flash or owl appearing unheard:
                              and

the rattler under the flare of the
redhawk which destroys the head first,
plucking out eyes and tongue: how

worrisome the yew-snow to the
she-cardinal, all day yesterday,
Sunday, stirred from her nest by boys playing

basketball, here this morning greeted by
another hassle: I hardly believe I don't
have to teach this morning: the first

Monday off: snow, free to draw winter
lines in the stickwork of tree and bush
inconvenienced inconveniences the midMay

boughs, so full and thin, catchy:
problem solvers subsidized with subsidies
and grants approach solutions but artists
dwell penniless with the central problem

41

we were talking about our MFA program
(pogrom) in Creative Writing when I said

should we, can we, professionalize
delight

and what better way to point up need
than by the superfluous

I said something like that, others
were saying other things, like why

not teach creative seeing or theory or the
voice of tone, or point-of-view

what I said was disrespectfully inane
and consequently useful to those

needing an angle offsight to true
up against, the clearing into range

of a blur: by the time my blur had
taken on the definition of balanced

variations and compromises it was
no longer delightful, and I turned

down everything clear, arranged for
small game: I do not care to hunt

if I cannot be run over by
an elephant or flushed out of the bushes

by an inquisitive lion or buttressed
with speed from the rear by a forward

waterbuffalo: I wouldn't want to kill
anything innocent unless it had

weaving in ranks before it a ridge of
cobras or dashing crocodiles: my

walking stick, I hope I said how it
makes me feel wooden about the

shanks when I go walking and dogs zoom
out to brag on their teeth: but it is

the very thing to challenge a dog or
man to violence: and if a man snatched

it away, it would become his weapon,
so effective and sufficient, against

me: what was said on this subject of
swords works for walkingsticks as well:

the moral nature of the North is such
it is considered indecent to be decent:

united we stand, divided we sit down:
once a month about I put everything

away, stickeraserbrush, paper, drafts,
inks, watercolors, clips, everything

away, clean up my room and walking out
declare, I am done with creativity,

only to discover the next day or hour
that everything cut down to

creativity everything goes with
that: I cut the grass, take up or

put in tulips, consider puttying up
the windowpanes, hack off some live or

dead branches here and there—but
come back to creativity and break

out all its gear again and set to
doodling: thank the Lord: home is

where the doodle is: today cleared
so bright blue one felt the offer,

this is it, take it, and trying to
take it found no way to do so: today

was a complete chance, a chance at the
complete, the adequate satisfaction:

how painful beauty is that gets away
full and unbesmirched and how comfortable

the rainy day that publishes your
lesser failures: life is roundabout

and roundabout and we are, with ups
and downs, linear: the round goes on

but we break in and out: the squirrel
killed 11 days or so ago, chucked off

the road by crow or cop, was chucked
back but right on the road's edge,

by the man cutting his lawn: several
days were cold and nothing touched

the squirrel and then the snow filled
his ear and tallied his tail out to

the feather bone: so he
is doing pretty good but the old

killing is still sketched on his face
and one wishes for the warm days,

the worms rising up under him and
draining him off into flight: I have

mourned him so many times I grow angry
at his self-ful staying on: disditches

42

minutiae is a fussy word
matrix is too perfect
often is often mispronounced
irregular suggests constipation
irregardless is one of those things
mucous is the nastiest slick on la lange
I like strut as in strutted veins
varicose moleways
    some people say they don't like
    thought flowing through illustrative
    images (they can't catch much)
    they prefer to dwell in one place into
    relevation unsuspected

everybody these days mixes up
lie and lay and mispronounces forehead

43

the high farm beseeches my mind,
thought, my mind soars up the hard
climb to the ridge but then
feels the backing of the ridge
to the sweep, the high passover
so laborious, everything under it
gentled, the still ponds, swallows
plinking them with fine lines, flies
spinning to burr shook into the surface
tension, nipper fish catching a
chink in the mirror informative as
a web: the earth is so fearful
and beautiful! ticks, mites,
flukes, spilldiddlings from the
assholes of filthy sheep—O
troubled shepherds—
I love nature especially if there's

a hospital nearby and macadam or
glass in between: or
the way it survives as cuttings
or seedlings in claypots or plastic
furrows cut off from the true ground: how
our forefathers hated woods and sex,
so much of both to deal with,
cut down or back: but now the
coonyus surrounded by taming
equations of the pill, the sperm
rage, such a wilderness, shot wild,
why we can horse deeply in with
irresponsibility's ease: that's what
they say: I'm afraid nature's going
to send the bill: it usually does:
ferocious tallywhacker

44

sweeps of space haunt the slopes,
the ridge starved to the wind that
skins it: boulders like springs
spill winter's coolth, residuals:
stones will not have warmed to summer
before frost cuts back: brook
stones cast shadows underwater,
deep in small falls' flow holes:
upland marshes, flow-slows, in them
logs idle, fallen den trees, turtles
big and little angle up the ascents
and sun a chill that won't come off

45

the thought that
so much is not wasted but is
the wellspring

of the tight usages we take
and spill! downridge from some spot
any way is ten miles, so much beneath
one one feels the invitational
unlidded, the not-held-down:
what smart fright! dive into the
fringes of houses on dirt roads, and
then paved narrow roads, and then
the main arteries, flowing a lot more
quickly, to the holding spleens of
towns by lakeshores low as you can get

46

culture, hardened to shellac's empty
usage, defines in definitions
hoaxdoms of remove from the true life
which
is smaller, leaner than a brook, no
louder, variable as, to the true rain:
the true life feels about its small
shoulders the traces and burdens of
death and turns for relief to berries,
bushes bent in abundance,
to dives into fell pockets of streams,
to musings on the clean forward edging
of the moon, to the eye of the other,
consolation, what there is, in the small
humbling touch

47

peeling the bark off a crabapple
cane, the purplepink woodskin, I heard
the loud oriole overhead in the maple
(looking for worms, I bet—we don't
have many this year, wonder why that

is, last year he could have opened
his mouth and a
bellyful would have crawled in, instead
he searched bough on bough, flying
and emitting scarves of music in
between, and never I think found a
thing)

worms ending in song

(except in the oriole's case one would
just as soon they didn't)

48

at dusk rabbits settle
out of the air and crop
the plumequill stems of blown dandelions
nibbling them up like drunk drinking straws
and then in the most delicate, short-range
leaps get over to the quince leaves
and trim the bush hind-leg high

49

little showers yesterday evening, quiet
as rabbits emerging into dusk to feed,
darkened the macadam except where

overhanging shower-holding trees drew their
negatives in dry ground: but this morning,
fog has built up drops in the branches and dripped

wet images of trees on ground otherwise dry:
needles and leaves collect until
their points bulge to drop and then if

the wind riffles a small shower will erupt
and rustle: fellow said he was so weak he
couldn't throw a shadow: maybe fog has

the multiplicity to deal with pollen, that
is, touch it in the air, grain to mist-drop,
and bring it down: but

on the first breeze that stirs
under a lifted fog, weavements and
shimmerings of pollen unlace

50

a light catches somewhere, finds human
spirit to burn on, shows its magic's
glint lines, attracts, grows, rolls
back space and dark, stands dominant
high in the midsphere, and reality
goes into concordance or opposition, the
light already dealing with darkness
designating it darkness, opposition by
naming, and the intensity of the source
blinds out other light: reason
sings the rightness but can do nothing
to oppose the brilliance: it dwells:
it dwells and dwells: slowly the light,
its veracity unshaken, dies but moves
to find a place to break out elsewhere:
this light, tendance, neglect
is human concern working with
what is: one thing is hardly better
or worse than another: the
split hair of possible betterment makes
dedication reasonable and heroic:

the frail butterfly, a slightly
guided piece of trash, the wind takes
ten thousand miles

51

I like nature poetry
where the brooks are never dammed up or
damned to hauling dishwater or
scorched out of their bottoms by acids:
the deep en-leafing has now come and
the real brook in certain bends dwells, its
stone collections dry-capped, shale shelves
in shade, leaves and falls murmuring
each to the other—and yesterday I
looked upbrook from the highway and
there flew down midbend a catbird to
the skinny dip, found a secure
underwater brookstone and began, in a
dawnlike conclave of tranquility, to
ruffle and flutter, dipping into and
breaking the reflective surfaces with
mishmashes of tinkling circlets.

2 TOMBSTONES

1

the chisel, chipping in,
finds names the
wind can't blow away

2

it breaks the heart
that stone holds
what time let go

but the stones are
the time left
that the names can be in

3

the ground flat or,
rolling from a hill rise, slightly
shedding,
no downpour can

organize flows to displace
the stones,
identifications tumbling
from one mound to another

4

set on the line between
time and abyss,
at the intersection
of usual time ongoing
and a time stopped within
other times,
the time of protons and electrons
going on as usual—a stone—
levels of existence
in existence, times
in time, one organization
gone still; otherwise,
nothing appears lost

5

the spirit, though, invisible,
weightless is lost: its
winding kept the winding
going: but only
winding when winding stops
disappears:
when one loses nothing one
loses everything

6

but why put a stone there:
we put a stone there
too heavy to build or fence with,
having no mineral content of value,
weighty enough
to hold time down,
a memorial, often without
recoverable recollection,
a deed to a million
facts, all missing

7

rivulets of scattering,
corruption's ways
of getting on with things,
rememberers unremembered,
still the name
will call together in the last
time, the new time, in the new morning,
all the bits of information and,
the name said,
the form will come again—the distance
between named and name run

8

dust's shape in air
could be a momentary
memorial, an instant signifying its interval,

that what is gone is
going on with other
going things,

a stability of motion
in time
accompanying its own time:

instead, a stone's
block
halts ongoing,

a blockage that says,
timelessness hereby measures
time going on as usual

9

the stone-name signifies
what it can find to mean
in some living head:
when the heads
are empty,
the stone's name names emptiness,
not the one
now neither a thing that is nor was

10

as if the name were not
already nothing,
stone, chipped away,

leaves the name nothingly
present,
grooves of absence

a further sign of a sign
that lightens
the anchorage of its carriage

11

the grooves fill with moss,
though, that spring
speaks green
and fall burns out with cold
into winter's black writing

12

a mockingbird sings to a whole
graveyard: the turbulence,
polishing the gravestones,
melts the names

13

the wind roars, sweeps, whirls,
nearly free even in its calms,
and the wind carries leaves, sand,
seed, whatever: rain pours,
puddles, flows: the ground
yields to this or that pull, break,
flush: among the swirling
motions, the stone's slow swirl
keeps the name

14

a stone sinks in soil like
a pearl in oil
or gathers sand and leaves
from the wind
to heap itself away:
or rain undermines a corner
and the name face
pitches to the ground
as if to call on
the deep for whatever rising
might raise it up again

15

when gliding perhaps under a glacier
or dissolving to bacteria and roots
the stone wears smooth
and can no longer keep the name,
will a clinging existence
give way, will an edge-fine
existence no longer exist

16

stones, names in them, are
just stones: when the stone
brushes mind, memory
changes the stone clear through

17

what does it matter if
a stone falls or slides and
misidentifies a mound:
the stone's outward
reference given up it
calls to itself

18

stones, as if forms of intelligence,
stir: concentrate light
still and you have them:

still, other durances exceed stones'—
a pulse in one of earth's orbits
beats once in four hundred thousand years:

in certain orders of time
stones blow by like the wind:
starlight pricks them like bubbles

19

the things of earth are not objects,
there is no nature,
no nature of stones and brooks, stumps, and ditches,

for these are pools of energy cooled into place,
or they are starlight pressed
to store,

or they are speeding light held still:
the woods are a fire green-slow
and the pathway of solid earthwork

is just light concentrated blind

20

the stone makes
its longest, hardest
"effort"
to hold on to, memorialize
the glint
or glow
once
in someone's eye

21

not coarse, hard
things last
longest, perhaps,

but fine, the very fine:
if only the wind
could take letters:

if only light
spelled names:
when love brushes

through our nerves
and sends
a summary to our brains,

perhaps the summary
is sent by
vibrations

really the universe's—
the universe, something as old as that
and with as much future

22

if love is fine
and stones are harsh evanescences,
how we may dishonor
love to letter down its name,
wasting the love
on the hard waters of inscription

23

the light in an eye
transfigured in
frames of feeling—

how is this small well,
so shallow and
deep, so magical

and plain able to
center all
the circumferences—

the eye itself
vision's vision
and visionary sway

24

the universe is itself
love's memorial,
every cliff-face,
rocky loft having
spent
itself through love's light,
here held
till love again burn it free:
ninety percent
of the universe is dead stars,
but look how the light still
plays flumes down
millennial ranges

25

nothing, though, not stone
nor light lasts
like the place I keep
the love of you in and this

though nothing can write it down
and nothing keep it:
nothingness
lasts long enough to keep it

26

if the tombstones were
thrown together in one pile,
that would be some gathering,
a record higher than
Everest:
but if time crumbled the stones,
washed out the grit,

melted down the shapes,
all the names distilled would
spell nothing

27

a flock of
gulls flew
by I thought but

it was a
hillside of stones

28

this boundary stone plunked down
with no answering
cornerstone, no three-stone
description of area, no field-square,
a point, dot
evaporated out of dimension,

but still a deep bound,
a boundary whorling deep

29

the letters,
holding what they can, hold
in the stone

but holding flakes or
mists away—a
grainweight of memory

or a rememberer goes:
in so many hundred years,
the names

will be light enough
and as if balloons
will rise out of stone

3 MOTIONS' HOLDINGS

••

Questionable Procedures

A bit of the universe's
business slopped
over and, strung
out of the way,
cooled and lode-slow
gave rise
here and there to
a quickness like
shade, protoplasm,
a see-through
coming and going of
dots and pulsing veils
that soon enough filled
the bit seas:
the veils and cauls
toughened, curled
into rolls, centralized
backbone: taking to
the land and coming up
into us, our agency,
they milled the
green continents white.

Frost's Foretellings

After fall, winds
rousing Halloween rains will
sometimes persist into
November

and on a halfmoon-bright night
dry the leaves and spool them
around, whirls
and spouts lifting them as if

to pencil the air the way
typhoons inscribe seas or
the ground, the leaves
skimming

rises clean and letting
go to slack fall
in hollows
or packing in along the roots

of catchment hedges:
the day drains down;
wind, time lean away
and

the leaves stiffen still,
all night taking on
the cold strick fur
snow can deepen and fill out.

20 January

Another day promised for forty
come and gone, and we're
still below freezing: but, at least,
the trees heavy with ice, it's
been calm: now, the gray deep
afternoon is turning windy, and

the thicket snaps like a fire,
ice creaking and jamming but
holding, an occasional splinter
at a crack flicking free:
another night enameled ghostly!
yesterday afternoon the sun broke

out late and the trees, perpendicular
to the light, lit up strict white
ice-lights at the fractures: tiny
stirs winked some: others held red, blue
glows, water-clear: tonight, we
have nothing to go on but continuance.

Early Indications

Are the warblers drifting
through, now, so many
plinks and squeaks, muttering

squishes and near
whistles in the bushes—
a wave bulging northward?

(my father called them
bloombirds—they came
treebloom-soon)

individual leaves flicker
even on the stillest days, the hedges
jumpy with a vision not quite

put together: some hours the
birds drift mute, fog-fine
driplets in a front:

their own score, they're the notes,
too, of a broader swell
the sun's all set to open with.

Loft

A sheet of shale chips
loose on my porch stoop
and its three hundred

million years, disrupted,
rise like plain ice-air
around me, thinning

the present time:
I spin the sheet
sheer in a long arc

to the yard's shrub bank:
the grain splinters and,
reentering,

sinks toward the foundation
of its next three
hundred million years.

Chiseled Clouds

A single
cemetery
wipes out
most
of my
people,
skinny old
slabs
leaning this
way
and that
as
in stray
winds,
holding names:

still, enough
silver
cathedrals fill
this
afternoon sky
to
house everyone
ever
lost from
the
light's returning.

Scaling Desire

A small boulder washed or
rolled down or out
of circumstance lay mid-desert,

a saltweed brittle in
rockshade
sleep beside it, roots

angled under for the deep cool:
the wind, rising to heat,
said

sit down by this big rock
and if in a year you're
still not bored, I'll show you

something really interesting:
but which way, I said, will
interest go, to rock only

or to showers
for the leafing saltbush:
or will you find me pavilions' banners,

silks, cushions, sweets—
the dew-soaked
roses of all longing.

Tertiaries

A starving man dreams of more than enough
and the thirsty man does not conceive
a drop: in a roomy, almost flawless nothingness,

I've made my abundance and, look, I still have
next to nothing, heaps of verbal glitterment,
rushes of feeling overrushing feeling:

you, well-founded in yourselves, have no
need of my show: keep away from it, it folds:
but how almost a true shower

illusion is for me and others of us,
the perishing: we enter into word-rain and
so closely think we live, we nearly live.

Upper Limits

As the snow
that had

the tan-spent
hydrangea

heads down upsidedown
melted,

the ground-bow
stems

ticked their
arcs away

as far as
they would

go up and straight,
and the wind's

gnarlings
pounced

on them
buffeting them

(though they
wouldn't stay)

higher than
they were

meant
to go again.

Laboratory Materials

Drag in the diseased and afflicted
to the meticulous observers
and they are fields of glory to be reaped
into knowledge heightened severe and memorable,
the clarity and reasonableness of
things gone wrong

but what is to be learned of the healthy person
he saunters in buoyant on a stack of splendor
to ask where to cart the next bad body off to:
meanwhile the diseased look up to receive
instruction in wall-eyed
astonishment bordering on bliss.

A Tendency to Ascendancy

Every day, I'm a foolish
man, misled: I have not only
my shambles but a shambles
of not knowing my shambles right,

but when the winds get too
high (like the high side
of a schizophrenia)
gulls

take to the air: beach worms move
at low tide to the deep bend
of their U-tubes
and other things make arrangements

if not to cure, to endure the siege:
I go over:
I assail the heights
and dwell in the continuous

sway of the mournful singing:
when matters lighten,
I fall & touch the ground,
re-recognize & lightly assume the ground.

Information Density

for Kenneth Burke

Generalization scans the contours of terrain
for the spot to take on concretion in,
the way a squirrel, having floated through

arches, zigzagged, digs for a nut, pear core,
or pats one in: generalization acquaints us
with the wider forms of disposition, airily

leaves out a lot in order to be cursory and
carries little substance so as to move big:
the squirrel pops erect, checks out the boughs

for dozing leapers, the bushes for stingers
snapping approaches, and waits to see if in the
chinks between branches a hawk's

roving connects dots into nearing curvatures,
then lets fall light forefeet and
nuzzles into the ground again: the world,

not everything, need not be less than
it is—animals thrive and fail in similar
problems of motion and risk, pull and haul:

the jay lights squalling right into what he wants:
the eagle wheels up in rigorous quiet, higher
and higher to find the right piece of ground.

Stone Keep

He sat down and
wept
  because there is neither saying
nor unsaying,

wept the sunlight
free of leaves,
  stitched up dandelions,
unsprinkled bluets,

broke birds'
songs down:
  everything going on
went on

over, though, on over
his cold keep:
  he hugged the heaving stone
tight.

Autonomy

I am living without you because
    of a terror, a farfetched
notion that I
can't live without you

which I must narrow down & quell,
    for how can I live
worthy of you, in the
freedom of your limber engagements,

in the casual uptakes of your
    sweetest compliances
if stricken in your presence
by what your absence stills:

to have you, I school myself
    to let you go; how terrible
to buy that absence
before the fragrance of any presence comes:

but though I am living without
    you, surely
I can't live
without you: the thought of

you hauls my heavy
    body up,
floats me around,
gives my motions point, just the thought.

Backcasting

I can tell by
the way
gravel will spill
through me some

day it's
all right to
mess around: I can
tell by the way

light will
find me transparent I
can't be gross:
I drift,

slouch about, spoof:
I true the
coming-before
to the consequence.

Checking out the Resources

Ice nearly meeting in the middle
has
drawn the brook out of sight

except for a central
ruffle that doesn't give
black glitter-winding up—imagine

a cold night's shelves of ice
knitted from the bank's
rubble and

held, pavilions, solid out over
the various disturbances
coming undone

to a few degrees of morning heat—
such waywardness, loss!
a dip rebuilds it overnight.

Dominion

Glittery river, I said,
rise, but
it didn't:

stop, then, damn
it, but it
didn't:

O river, I said,
ruffle
blurring

windknots up
(and
that was nice

like perch striking roils
at surface
flies):

river, I said, don't
turn back,
and it eased on

by,
majestic in the sweetest
command.

Hairy Belly

I don't take brooks seriously
but you could say if a brook's dry
it's stopped running or

gravity's off—I don't
take verse seriously but
if it moves inaccurately

potholes appear in the street:
they say: I may take verse
less seriously than that:

gravity, though, isn't that
a weak-field force: verse is:
but prevalent: it dwells along

the shale edges in brook-ripples' shadows:
the shadow of vine-threads is a
good place: also, though, it

dwells in the special activity
of chloroplasts' vine-skin
cells along the sunny

line: but I don't take
vines over brooks or defining
shale ledges too seriously: still,

if chloroplasts didn't jiggle-knit
spinning in sunny cells, your
lips' scarlet would not be scarlet long.

Entranceways

If not ready to
go, to be gone

I looked about
at the heightenings leavetaking

confers, things
abstracted

useless stricken
new:

perhaps, I thought,
I will finally

be here
in going's final syllable,

compensations idealizing,
departure entry:

but then the hunger,
say, for trees,

pear trees, the old
mellow wood,

the snow, sprouts,
a tree,

to turn around
and see,

to feel, just as
the fingertip

vanishes, to whirl
back, having learned how to

stay just as one is
swept away.

Dominant Margins

If the universe is spilling one
way (favoring this or that) it is

local abberation a brief time
formation controls

for in the high places where the
middling finest balances work

equilibrium shimmers like any
lack of trouble in a still of mirrors:

oh, if one is skeptical and smart
and sees through the boxes of

practice the blank beyond of disbelief,
he needs mercy's help for the knowing:

but, on the other hand, to waken
in an ultimate extremity, death or love,

to a reveille bleaching out the colorful
pennants of belief!—a predicament

underpinning will have few resources
to rescue one from: but if you

sit still (there's a name for that)
balancing and unbalancing move

aside: among the leanest
gaps of value, a tiny motion,

narrow and fast, so fine it scorches
your hands with having it or not

having it, a catchball of gusts
too indeterminate to name, invisible

and practically imperceptible anyhow,
there's a difference (where there

is hardly any) there's a difference
going one way or the other.

Power Plays

I know that splendor's your
arms, your hands,
not spools and drifts of stars:

your hair, falling, gives in
the way desire builds defenseless:
you soothe my twists; unwinding,

they wind into your calm:
don't be afraid: deference
controls me: I can

win or lose you and find
the bone in your arm
still too fine to bear.

Target

In spring the high twig tip
puts out a blur that,
if not undershadowed, represents

itself below with a
correspondent invention on the ground:
the sun lengthens

drawing longer and longer northerly
arcs
until the leaf, if not undershadowed,

declares its full singular shape:
the sun eases back wintering
south

and the high
leaf, acorns cracking,
dives into its shadow running on the ground.

Postulation

I place my *be* down,
but it
buzzes as on a
hotplate: I lift it,

a clear
drop, and
place it shining down
again, but

it steams and stews:
be, I say: it runs:
be, I say: it
hisses dry.

Subsidiary Roles

I said to the brook stones
(rock brightest and most
available) you aren't,
mute and drowned shallow,

showing us what saying
comes to, a rush
in the underrush of silence:
I said, don't take

away illusion, the aspiration
that saying chips
room out of necessity's
lidded hard lot:

and don't, I said, going
right on, don't
come out dry, turtle-dull
in a dry spell, and

surface-babbling as
if for rain, show
us still
more convincingly what saying changes.

Working Out

It boom-a-loomed
& bam-a-lammed
last night in

the high-towered
flash-lit hours
after midnight

turning by daybreak
into
meditation-like rain:

celestial tensions
grounding,
electron clouds

swarmed up hills,
funneling up trees,
to arc with heaven:

I grumbled to
sleep and the Japanese
beetles

newly arrived
on the blanched
green Siberian

elm leaves
that came out
where the doe

fed in the yard last
month must have
shined

bronze-green through
the blue-bronze
highlightings.

Remembering Old Caves

I think I'd like to die in the woods,
not wode, I mean, but wandered,
lost from the table drains,

embalmed arteries, away
from musty music, plastic carpets,
and the softness

of the spoken word: imagine
being walked off halfdead by kinsmen
and left slumped by

a log or rock, the screams already
on you or certain to come on
with night, friends turned back

caveward and all the wailing probably
attracting a big one that might not
kill you before lugging you off, though.

Becoming Become Of

It's a clear case with rivers—
they're going to go on with the ongoing;
otherwise, darters headed upstream

would have no currency to keep true-still in:
parasites and speckled snails that ride on
struck fronds or unshucked coconuts

wouldn't float free to colonizations elsewhere:
riverweeds on wharf legs would flop sail-dull,
not dancing and pointing downstream where the action went.

Holding Sway

I waited for the robin, fluffing
and preening on a long branch

of honeysuckle, to fly off
so I could see by the lift how

much his sway was, when a catbird
landed on the branch, farther out,

and that was a deep sway! then
the robin flew, lifting the catbird

a little, and then the catbird
flew away, the branch springing up

pretty nicely: by subtracting the
catbird low from the two lifts

and guessing (by how much the catbird
had risen to the robin's flight)

where the branch must have been
before the robin first came, I got

a good notion how close it came to
where it, then, was and how

much the robin had
first brought down the branch.

The Dwelling

I would as soon believe
in paradise as in
nothing: it is no great

wonder that our spiritual
energy, purified, returns
to, is, the eternal

residence: no greater
wonder than that earth is
here at all: imagine

arriving on this green
curvature and being spent!
and no great wonder that

the eternal residence is
a place nothing wants to
stay in, but only, from

the terrifying, exciting
confusions working energy
sharp, to return to:

belief's a fine cloth:
a sheen before the eyes,
it induces fabrications

ash can't get to and just
residual energy composes:
let belief down somewhere,

I say, the heart's cravings
flaring bright into near
exemplifications: this

jewelry of brick and loft,
at least!—until ready for
the greater knowledge, the

greatest, perhaps, we accede
to reason that here the plainnest
majesty gave us what it could.

The Hubbub

Just as the lesser gods, local,
imbalanced into activity,
loosened from wholeness into the efficacy
of partiality and preferment,

just as the lesser gods, deriving
their powers from a stiller, higher
source, may suggest clearer
networks we can

appeal our wishes to, so we ourselves
find helpful confinement in
smallish dispositions, pushing
severe thought aside at times to

fix dinner or giving up the sweets
of trance a minute
to help guests shuffle off big
coats and snow boots:

divinity's loftier stations can worsen
one,
apprehensions that take hold so,
shuddering and shivering

at being stilled, break out
in their midsts: sitting still in
contact with the central formless
seems worthiest as some, perhaps

imagined, alternative to the roil
of time, frittering and fracturing
us sharp across surf-surfaces:
whereas being still inside,

having found a token or tidbit of safety
(where, though, and how are such
trifles when they are needed found—
in forced alternatives?)

enables us to grab the sailmast
and skim storm waves nearly at the wind's force,
supreme pleasure in the
speediest plunge and flare:

lessened down far to the trivial,
energyless, casual;—empty stances,
paradisal with indolence, sweeten
to a sweetness savorless on high.

Abstinence Makes the Heart Grow Fonder

Midnight moonlight chisels the eaves' icicles blue
but it's so parched cold and
late, the moon

shriveled sharp, the light splits
into a dozen
dazzles per eaves-tooth—

the raccoon waggles through the
hedge tunnel and on off gritty over the glittery
snow crust

checking out the garbage routes,
his head down in a trance of cold,
lacking scent:

it's time to give the spectral magic up, let
the eaves' jewel-work go to waste:
it's into Sunday morning and not a can is out.

Red Shift

My begonia blossoms are
pale as a speleologist's
windpipe, this winter

a cave's clouds we've been
traveling in: but, now,
the end of January is

breaking the sky into shale
the sunlight cracks through:
I'm moving the begonia

closer up to the window:
when the freeze-foliage
on the panes burns off, the sun

will draw bright blood back into blossom.

Saving Spending

My little way
though the
least way is

of the same way
(assimilation and surprise)
as any

though it can
go
on, I suppose,

branching, only
a little way:
but out to

its twiggiest
end, perhaps, curlicues
of its directions

survive &
loosening waywardly
find their

way back to
a
new way that

radiantly
roves or slightly
abandons the universe.

Long Sorrowing

My path's so
frail it's
hardly discernible

from
wilderness: no
gravelway

laid and no
signs up:
brookbanks are

unmodified for crossings,
the flies ghastly:
but when I

tire I take up
backing with
a boulder too old for any event

and doze and
listen for
existence

in its
water-like
deep,

the voices of
ciliates & crustaceans
among

tracings and fernprints
held in a dark unanswerableness
to so much loss.

Eidos

On those late March afternoons
when a flurry nearly rain
eases over and the few big

flakes, old flies, stall,
lift, dive, sweep in a slow
loose-knotted breeze, I watch

the lineations of the dance, air's
least-holding script, whose
figures carve on my retina

motions the mind mulls over
and subdues to
intelligible reticula, informing shapes.

White Passages

Peaks and rivers, cold
soggy passes, declivities,
willows
in the quartermoon river bends,

stalk-dead
row
willows high, moon-chalky

at floodline:
sparrows
light on, walk out on

weedstalks to bleak heads'
enormous swaying,
skinny clouds running
the sun moonwhite.

A Way Away

Some spring thunderstorms, blunderingly
following on thaws, are so breezy

they get an old leaf
up that falling into updrafts

can't get down:
the wind will, leaping

out of held moil, lift
the leaf higher than did any

tree
and the leaf in the chancy

currents will wobble
like a butterfly

and gravity will seem to lose
trace of it, and it will

angle up till wandering off you
forget to notice if it ever lands.

Pots and Pans

So what if the reality
out there's inert
(though the brook flows on)
until

imagined and, imagined,
changed,
transfused and
tinctured,

made out
in glassy, mirroring
human separations:
still, the ground base

appears much more
differentiated than
brook shale or grist tailings,
the reality

out there includes,
as we suppose,
have gained the careful
intricacy

to suppose,
consequential and random
sequences, organizations
into high points

from which all men may
at whatever height
of imagination learn:
unless there is a place,

where is such a
place and how
could it be,
empty, paradisal,

a still point from
which, all things
come together,
radiance glimmeringly

emerges, or more
deeply, from which
the coming in
and going

out of things has
lost distinction:
then the reality
found there, empty,

seems like a place
the mind made
though the mind
imagines it found it

there first and
then perceiving it
"came into it"—
rippling gamelans

build imperceptible
stillnesses
just over their
bongs and

clinks, an emptiness
as of figured
light, a permanence
the mind's home.

Aquarium Watch

Surfaced, the snail pokes
a tube into the air
and takes in a shell full:
when he gets too much
and, let go to sink,
floats, trapped weightless,
he measures and measures,
as if studying, then
tilts and a single
sized bubble escapes the shell rim:
and down he goes, as if
dreaming gravity's smoothest dream.

Earliest Recollection

Thaws snow-clear the fields
and woods, and leaves
snow's small weight

touched down last fall
crinkle to the breezes
and rise gathering dry

to dash about, whirl
with the liveliness
of the dead re-winded,

the end of stories not their
story's end,
everything

else too naked to
swish or starkly sway and
nothing else free to travel.

Liquidities

The biosphere waterbased
figurations here—
leaves, flies, flakes—
durance is as it were

uphill against the wind,
prolificacy profligate,
prolix strewings like
showers shedding windy out

of spruce woods after storm
(though it's only spring,
already showers
from the tiny-seeded maple

of goldenheaded tadpoles,
woven tails sprinkling
wet asphalt)—staying
is offish, dropping into

underbrush of established
woods, the chance a
chance blow will
twist something rotten off

or a fire quick clear
shading out density of limb
and vine—or even if
chance allows the hold

life, the crest of the
hill comes, the wind shifts,
gravity pulls the heldback
motions apart, the motions water.

Surgeons

The debranching foot-wide wound
that lightened the big siberian
elm has mooned into
the second summer,

shiny with sap and slick
meal lanky
worms and maggots have,
tunneling, mapped

and beetles have
stood sipping
in: but yesterday's
damaging winds and

downpour scrubbed the wound
scum-clean, and now
the old news
of its

growth shines in staffs
of round music
bright to exact count's
interval and ring.

Motion's Holdings

The filled out gourd rots, the
ridge rises in a wave
height cracks into peaks, the peaks

wear down to low undoings whose undertowing
throws other waves up: the branch
of honeysuckle leaves arcs outward

into its becoming motion but,
completion's precision done, gives
over riddling free to other

motions: boulders, their green and white
moss-molds, high-held in moist
hill woods, stir, hum with

stall and spill, take in and give
off heat, adjust nearby to
geomagnetic fields, tip liquid with

change should a trunk or rock loosen
to let rollers roll, or they loll
inwardly with earth's lie

in space, oxidize at their surfaces
exchanges with fungal thread and rain:
things are slowed motion that,

slowed too far, falls loose, freeing debris:
but in the ongoing warps, the butterfly
amaryllis crowds its bowl with bulbs.

Burnout in the Overshoot

The first cool spell has
cracked the white asters open,
samples here and there,

and tomorrow's promised warmth will
stir a few bees loose:
there's something besides

death and nothingness
even if winter is coming:
and, anyway, death isn't

a place you get all the way
to: as you arrive
what is arriving

diminishes and
finally, touch to touch,
nothing is equal to nothing.

Telling Moves

The hawk before the dusk storm
drops into,
rounding out a stoop

the same
as ever, but I'm
no longer true:

the willow's gold's green again,
wept branch-withes
floating as if

away on gusts, flared
fountains, but I'm
not getting things right:

the old fall
off in a doze or,
frozen to a kind of interest,

meet the pain presentably,
but I'm
not standing out in any clearing:

hawk and willow, the stilt-right
arrivals of the old:
the grave, I cannot accept it,
there is no way to give it up.

Coming Round

The oar squeaks,
a dash sound like
moon-hustle on the river:

reeds
trap and ease the
boat slow

to ripple-tilting sanddown:
the night, a
bubble,

hangs two hundred
thousand miles by
a moon-filament:

I tie up, head for the single
windowlight:
I cut the moon free.

Recoveries

The universe loosens, disperses,
dissolves away until its
veils, drifted fine, sway entangling

on themselves into new knots
of concentration & high
condition: meanwhile, in the

immediate system shelving
away, there must be constant
throwing off, cutting back

to hold the firm
defined: genetic material's
extravagant loss along the

edging peripheries of accident,
poor formation, mischance,
unwholesome surprise must be

defended against, compensated for—
where does the tiny whining,
insisting energy come from that

sings stuff back together,
resilient threads, bends, promoting
shape through time: though

the universe is dissolving,
minor countermotions mix
out from which are derived

flares of form, modes of slim
continuance, mounting
lofts, mingling seed.

Trivial Means

We don't want to be just
the narrows or shambles through which
great motions make their way:

we want to know why or how
the motions stirred first
and whether their moves are

prefigured or moment-to-moment
providentiality and surprise:
we make capability's show

of discerning outline,
of recognizing and measuring
true, and we don't understand why,

servants to flesh, we must also
subserve realization, knowing no
more than we find out and only when

we can, death merely breaking us
away from that: the elements don't reply,
not on a day like this,

wide openness the blue cage, though
they jar at times, report, drown,
strike: this language spoken in
lives under overpassings of necessity.

Tracing Out

What buoys the butterfly,
the world's
weight, I project: slow
motions of the bleakest

metals and stones
suggest, like an
intelligence, the undeniable
possibility; on that,

the wind,
thread muscles and plastic
joints, the butterfly jounces:
but lightness, like making

sense, is just more of
the world's weight
momentarily fined:
tissues of sense, spun out

of sense filaments,
become clumpy trees, roll
jungles under: bound way away:
the world's weight's the world's.

Some Any

What do you have if you can't waste it,
what good is it if you have to dam it
up to dip it out,
what is anything worth if not so

common it isn't worth anything,
why fool with anything so scarce you
have to be grateful for it,
why if surprised you had a thought today

bother to think at all
when the thought is as best itself
plentiful and dirt cheap,
why love at all if diminishing love you

have only enough for Tuesday,
who needs anything he really needs,
where could the necessary be found if
not anywhere where where

Memory

When everything is leveled off
even with the ground
    will a brier or reed
figure
us up to the light again:

where so little's made of
difference
    will we
recover immortality's mindfulness
in a shoot's leaf:

from indifference will we
put together enough
    yearning
to gouge the dark loose: or when
sand skins the ground

will no knowledge of loss be in it
and in the wind no wailing.

Sight Seed

When the jay caught
the cicada midair, a fluffy,
rustling beakful, the
burr-song flooded dull but
held low: the jay perched and
holding the prey to the branch
as if to halt
indecorous song pecked
once, a plink that did it,
but in the noticeable silence
proceeded at ease
and expertly to
take this, then that eye.

Negative Symbiosis

Without linkage or
ravin living
couldn't
last: however
far through
changes

the gnat wrestles
the bulby
high
evening air;
however far
into the

dark the worm
rubbles
under the root,
life takes a
bow,
gives

the go-ahead:
even the
rattler,
his neck
gagged with
fur,

trims up
the world so
something
tiny can
come
through.

Citified

You can turn goats loose on an island
and forget about fences: your
chickens can graze away from the yard

and not stray: your horse or cow can
range wide securely: the land
ends in all directions, and surf marshals

the shore tight: but much as an island
prevents escape it welcomes entry and no
eye can watch the round at once: glance up

at the horizon's flat line
but what on the island's
other side is oozing or clamoring ashore,

a sea novelty or a pestilence of
demonstrable mouths: your horse
could screech, your cow low, your goats

whirl, huff, and stamp, the unfenced
becoming the line of defense, alert line,
at least: and guineas, if you had any,

could chatter day or night to the unusual:
but roundly enclosed just so
roundly vulnerable, you might as well live in

a single small direction, splinter, among others'
fractures and have to look nowhere but ahead
except of course occasionally to glance behind.